PRAISE FOR *PERFECTA*

In *Perfecta*, Patty Seyburn continues her one-of-a-kind witchery, casting spells that bind the humorous to the philosophical in ways that look headlong at the living world and make use of every inch of it. From winding, discursive poems that question her own passions to short lyrics that give lovely little eye-rolls to her unrelenting obsessions, *Perfecta* is at once personal and transcendent, joining the politics of dinner parties and lines from Hass and Biblical allusion and the memory of Detroit. After reading this book, I want to make something.
—Jericho Brown

Flummoxed and fraught, beset by free will, the characters who populate Patty Seyburn's fabulous poems live like us. They apply for jobs, they eat out, they bike, they raise kids, they hate clowns—they do what we do, only with the confidence of Plato, which means skeptically. Smart, funny, and quizzical, this Seyburn: soaring, gorgeous, and frightened, these poems. Brava.
—Alan Michael Parker

Not too many people could figure out a way to be hilarious about ancient Greek philosophy, but for Patty Seyburn it's a walk in the park, or perhaps, a ball hit out of the park, as are so many poems in *Perfecta*. What I love most about them is that they're pure Seyburn: full of her inimitable, quirky, funny and affecting voice. No one else would imagine a mathematically minded brother "in another life . . . run [ning] around with some kook like Pythagoras or Newton," or point out, in discussing the use of a stone for a pillow, "that's what Jacob used/ and he slept fine," or give us wide-reaching statements from "time emits a foul smell if you ask me" to "the gifted and talented are gullible." But these seeming wisecracks— unforgettable as they are—can't possibly convey the scope of this terrific book. You'll simply have to read it.
—Jacqueline Osherow

WHAT BOOKS PRESS

AN IMPRINT OF

THE GLASS TABLE

COLLECTIVE

LOS ANGELES

ALSO BY PATTY SEYBURN

Hilarity
Mechanical Cluster
Diasporadic

PERFECTA

PATTY SEYBURN

WHAT
BOOKS
PRESS

LOS ANGELES

Publisher's Cataloging-In-Publication Data

Seyburn, Patty, 1962-

  Perfecta / Patty Seyburn.

   pages ; cm

  ISBN-13: 978-0-9889248-5-7

  ISBN-10: 0-9889248-5-4

  1. American poetry. I. Title.

PS3569.E88637 P47 2014

811/.54

What Books Press
363 South Topanga Canyon Boulevard
Topanga, CA 90290

WHATBOOKSPRESS.COM

Cover art: Gronk, untitled, mixed media on paper, 2014
Book design by Ash Goodwin, ashgood.com

PERFECTA

CONTENTS

Time is a great teacher, but unfortunately it kills all its pupils.

Hector Berlioz

STICK & STONES

Back in the day, matter spread out in a nearly uniform sea
with subtle undulations.

Over time, gravity pulled matter into vast filaments
    filament, filament, filament

and emptied the intervening voids.
Cosmic acceleration has changed all that: no clumping.

We go too fast!
I've had trouble with my cake mixes clumping.

For centuries, the process changed little.
    pat-a-cake, pat-a-cake

The 16th century Spice Cake, the 18th century Nun's Cake,
even the rich Pound Cake of our colonial days required

long hours of labor, which Puritans enjoyed—each suffering
just another correction on the sinuous path to the afterlife.

    spare the rod
Balaam's ass refused to continue along his path because

he saw an angel blocking his way, holding a sword.
He swerved three times—the last was really a crouch—

and nothing could tempt him to budge.
Ass and snake are the only talking animals in scripture.

The Garden abundant with what we now call "produce."
blackberry, blackberry, blackberry

It does not say when God created stones.
nine days old

Jacob slept on one for a desert-pillow.
David readied five smooth for Goliath

who fell and the Theory of Improbability was born.
was enough to make a man stare

This spawned the phrase, "What are the odds?"
This begat the track and the trifecta

which demands you pick three horses in order.
Praising his mistress's disheveled appearance,

Robert Herrick wrote the poem, "Delight in Disorder."
and a merry old soul was he

Disordered states outnumber ordered ones.
Order is a first-class luxury like certain fowl.

    duck, duck
Bobby Fischer spends time in Japan playing random chess.

Back-row pieces are rearranged to eliminate what he calls
the "yawning predictability" of the game.

Fischer is a jerk.
Really, a jerk.

    had a wife and couldn't keep her
Newton thought gravity always attractive but now

we've found that some is repulsive, though I don't like to judge.
I do like to listen to my son sing, as infants have perfect pitch.

spoil the child
Soon, I tell him, you will get your own stick and you can poke

the devil in the eye.
three blind mice, three blind mice

The earliest printed books are called *incunabula,* from the Latin
for "swaddling clothes."

This is where the colophon comes from.
I have an affection for symbols because they take up so much

less room than the phenomenal world.
little lamb, little lamb, little lamb

Still, I would rather not fall from a great height.
let down your hair

It can be hard to put me together.

THAT WAS THEN

I would watch the great beetles
climb a local trellis.
Their steadfast journey served as a salve
to what ailed me.

They never digressed, invested
in the process of ascent and descent,
a completed gesture.

I am often guilty of sullen behavior,
and wrestle not with angels
but lesser matters, and tend
to sever my efforts

before achieving an end.
Poor me, you.
Bug. Scaffold.

This is my salvo over
mortality's bow,
confession of sins so ordinary,
they don't add up, even performed

with great constancy.
Wait. I also lie, keep
grudges in my pocketbook and try

too often
to create a brutal symmetry.

THE CASE FOR FREE WILL

When I was little, I thought the moon was Europe.
Or was like Europe.
Or would be like Europe, by the time I grew up.
Exotic, and far, but not impossibly far—we would go there
on vacation, once or twice, and learn about other cultures,
those that spawned ours—some of which died like
19th century mothers in childbirth.
By that time we would have found culture on the moon
and the moon's culture would be something like Europe's:
many museums with familiar paintings and sculptures,
canals and vast churches, old stone edifices,
gaudy commercials, bitter coffee and crusts of bread
and couture and whores in the windows
with Yma Sumac piped in.

ii.

It's early enough in the day to pursue
other interests, like bass fishing and shopping for overpriced objects.
Or, you could get a cup of coffee and brood as to why
joy eludes you at every turn, and you turn
quite a bit.
Consider how limitless the world seemed
when Armstrong landed his prodigious foot in that weird
powder and bounced along from there.
Houston, the Eagle has landed.
Let's take a dip in Tranquility Bay.
The astronauts, like gods, didn't comment on their feelings
or suggest a course of action. They were too busy
collecting rocks after uttering a scripted sentence missing an article
and pushing that symbol into terra incognita.

iii.

I was awake but not too aware back then.
Vietnam in my living room
but I missed the casualties.
I missed my father's heart attack, recovery.
I missed the Shelby Mustang, and the drumroll of assassinations.
Bound to leave my home, and not return.
Have you seen the pictures of the Saturn 5 separating?
Stage from stage, until the lunar module and lunar lander are completely
on their own.
Get me out of this atmosphere!
Having done their part, they are dispensable.
If you think that happiness is a matter
of expectations fulfilled, think again.
That's the only bad habit I ever picked up.

iv.

And still there's the moon: half-dark, half-light,
never making us more welcome than on that first visit.
How does it expect to be like Europe?
People want to feel wanted and there is competition: that hotbed, Mars.
Saturn, with those more than cocktail-party-distance rings.
And Venus, who seems close, beckons
but gives not an inch: tease and tart of the cosmos.
The planets cannot help what they are, locked
in orbit. Can we?
Before age five, I had free will.
William James said: *My first act of free will shall be to believe in free will.*
After, destiny took over, and everything I decided
in the most labored fashion, was already
coded in the stars.

v.

Poor stars.
Rich stars.

STOP THE CLOCK

I spent most of my time
in the contrary. *Mary, Mary.*
Now I live in the Yes, Sure.

If you must take me back,
let's return to that cruel pool game,
blind explorers in the deep,

displacing small waves,
desperate to touch anyone:
Marco! Polo! Marco Polo!

PERFECTA

My big brother took me to the track.

He was a grown up.

I was a child.

I split two-dollar bets with my sister-in-law.

Two on Hell-To-Pay, please, mister, I'd say at the betting window.

Two on Siren's Song, Silk Stockings, Who's Your Daddy, Barbie's Dream.

Horses' names are always like that: sort of obvious.

Names reflect namers: who they are or want to be.

I strode up to the window, cheerfully.

Always polite.

No one ever said: where's your mama?

No one ever said: how old are you?

My brother showed me how to read the racing form.

It was very mathematical. Categorical.

My brother loves numbers.

In a different life he'd have solved Fermat's Theorem, or run around with some kook

like Pythagoras or Newton.

You pick your horses based on how well they've done until now.

You wouldn't place a bet on some unproven new kid

unless you know something about him.

Maybe they have the hot trainer.

Maybe their owner owns winners.

Maybe their sire was a legend.

Remember that Lou Reed song? "What becomes a legend most?"

Remember Lou Reed?

Or maybe, you just have a "feeling" about the horse.

Maybe he's dappled, and you liked the word "dappled."

This all comes back to me now, and I haven't been for decades.

I can still see the tiny print.

Then I could read it.

There are people at the track with broken faces and fingers.
People who drink and dope and smoke.
People who throw their money at lost causes with funny names
because a longshot really pays off
especially in a perfecta or a trifecta.
People with a penchant for debt, and an allergy to winning.
People with coded gestures.
People named Sal.
I could never pick the order in which horses would win.
I'd feel lucky if my horse showed some pride, some chutzpah.
I thought, for a kid, I had the knack.
My sister-in-law and I usually broke even:
we were cheap dates.

My other brother took me horseback riding at a farm outside of the city.
The city was closer to the country, then.
My horse ran into the woods as I gripped its mane.
Galloped and galloped while I held fast.
My knees gripped, too.
Every part of me: gripped.
Branches scratched my face and arms.
My sister-in-law's horse wouldn't move after mine bolted.
They were siblings or friends.
Or simply used to following each other.
It's a beautiful story.
The whole processional stopped.
Apparently, I got the wild one.
Give the city kid the wild one—that'll show her.
God has a funny plan.
The guide caught up to me after what seemed like years.
What was years was how long I had nightmares.
I'd dream that my horse ran through endless woods, ending up at I-75.
And my parents would pass in the Ford LTD, en route to Flint or Tampa, and
see me,
but they couldn't catch me, and I wanted them to.
It was no use.

I was on that horse for good.
I was later embarrassed to learn what Freud said about horses.
Horses and girls.
My poor brothers: both complicit in some inevitable rite of passage.
Unintentionally.
They're fine men.
They wanted to get to know the little girl who was their sister
when they were already men, with lovely wives.
They invited me into their lives, and I shyly accepted.
I wonder what will give my daughter her nightmares.
What fun excursions I'll dream up or allow
that will make her bolt up in bed, sweating.
Night after night, for years
until she learns that if it wasn't one fear,
it would be another.
Something will take her away.
I don't gamble.
Correction: I have children.
I don't go to the track or casinos.
I stay far away from Vegas, the slots, cards, craps, sports.
What I don't know about myself is legion.
I don't want to find out the hard way.
Let's just say that temptation wears Italian loafers you can't afford.
Let's just say he drives some old-model Jag that you'd look good in.
That anyone looks good in.

Remember that time at the Mirage?
I read some elaborate explanation for mirages.
It's all about expectations: when conditions are right, the brain assumes
water must be present, along with the sky.
The brain is a dreamer.
The brain leaps to a false, wishful conclusion.
The brain will arrive there, over and over.

THE PLAN FOR TODAY

This morning we are going to test beds.

What do you need from a bed?

Some meet your back, fill you in
at the knees, neck, ankles.

Adapt to your indents and excesses.
On your side, they cradle you.

At the edge, they keep you
from falling.

Some yield, and some push back.
Some are unrelenting.

They say: we are good for you.
And pleasure is good, in a different way.

Some have continuous
springs, and some

individual.
The former will let you feel

another person get into your bed.
The latter will make you each discrete:

you can choose
or not

to acknowledge
the beloved or at least

the one who lies next to you
each night.

Most
nights. Lie
down. Roll around. Stretch. Reach out.
There is now technology inside of

a bed, which used to be
such a simple thing:

something soft atop
something hard.

Before that: just something hard:
a flat stone. Flat dirt. A smaller flat

stone for a pillow.
That's what Jacob used

and he slept fine.
(Not really:
he dreamed a great deal.)
His dreams felt real.

God and angels invaded his dreams. Made demands.
Mine are parochial. Predictable.

Perhaps a new bed would
solve that.
Perhaps I would dream bigger.
Even, prophetically.

How long should this bed last?
How long will the dreams

go on?

A CRY, THE CATALYST

and though the source seems far
it becomes so, as the proscenium
and your bit part continues
critic. The only thing we all have
once in our sleep, for Who
some ancient plant, the panacea
and engraved the voice's signature
a noise to give even the wise lover
into rest and restlessness, and while
than the *genius loci,* the echo of no
to others, despite our claims of
and the angels, droning cynics,
to tell your fortune, if you can
terrible guises and you do not
pretty, pretty, pretty? Even now
is current. Even now I dream it

from elusive, on dwelling
of possibility fills with players
to survive the Pedant's inner-
done is muttered, whimpered
Can Heal All or Her talisman—
with pallid leaves and curious stem—
upon the entablature of night,
pause. From there our ways digress
we long to be nothing less
memory we made tethers us
separation. Call out by day
will ignore you. Implore Proteus
hold him while he assumes
let go. You think the future is
I know the imagined cry
and it becomes legend.

THE PITCH

I can save you time and money, he said.
Nothing more. How could I resist?

Wipe your feet on the carpet, I said, thinking
he might end up erasing the prints with

a fine powder ground by mortar and
pestle, activated by a blow-torch: magic!

Instead, he sat on my divan like a man
who believed in his product and I said,

whatever you're selling, I'm buying
before he could launch into his shpiel.

He complimented me on my beagle.
Fine breed, he said. *The best,* I agreed.

*So agreeable and nice to neighboring
kids. Kids make it all worthwhile,* he said

and before I knew it, we were slapping
our thighs with joy, sharing those stories

of our offspring—the ones where they
scare you to death with some childish

prank you taught them or narrowly avoid
a jail sentence—and drinking that brandy

I'd been saving for a colicky day when
all that seemed to want doing would be

listening to the melody of skidding
wheels on blacktop while stones skipped

along the gutter. Then it was time
for lunch and he stood up, a bit abruptly,

I thought, considering, and asked for
a glass of water, which he drank while singing,

"Bess, You Is My Woman Now," proving
that ventriloquism is not dead

outside of the Standard Metropolitan
Statistical Area including Las Vegas.

We said farewell in a European fashion
inappropriate within 300 miles of Rockford

before he went on his way to his next
appointment, a big account, his bread

and butter, his meat and potatoes and I said,
well, I sure hope they feed you! and we laughed,

the morning one more figment of history.

DAYS OF 1984

We would light a cigarette to make the El
       round the track's curve—
you could have one or the other, smoke or ride,
       (dioscuri of the habitual),
and the first invites the second, tease/taunt
       the lesser gods
of small desires, regent and viceroy of ritual.
       We would drink
Louis Gluntz' Rouge, Blanc, and *Egri Bakaver*—
       Bull's Blood—in courtyard—
apartments with eroded pissing-boy fountains,
       dissolute Cupids true
to myth—debauched, perverse—where we kissed
       the wrong people,
deceived one another and apologized ferociously,
       word trumping deed,
faith over acts though we'd exiled all creeds to
       Fort Lauderdale on spring break.
We would kick streetlamps to make them go
       on, off, and steal
the white-food casseroles of roommates from upstate
       New York who rehearsed
being broke while waiting for their big break, slender
       as reeds despite
the economy of starch: *I bend and break not,*
       wrote La Fontaine.
We would down grain-alcohol punch lovingly
       ladled by charming
Sigma Phi Chi Alpha Psi Omegas, cheat
       at 8-ball in rec rooms,

revere the bad advice of bands with dead
        members, opine, recline,
learn the etiquette of embarrassment, leave
        very late, late
indeed, walking home while one person steered
        a bike serpentine
in overcranking Noh slow-motion, sober angel,
        furtive and fervent, staving
off the three sisters, furies of suburban darkness
        who'd punish our petty
misdeeds (misdemeanor carelessness and cruelty)
        while we woozily tilted
at windmills with stuttered rhetoric from the survey
        course of our charismatic
Marxist professor refused tenure: class, everything
        is class. We would sleep
in our narrow beds and in our friends' narrow beds
        and on the couch, any
couch and in any loft, and any food after 2 a.m.
        was nectar in neon served
with nightshift tolerance, dawn flaring
        in our saucers.
We would watch grim or flippant
        French or German films
on dates not dates, all nuance and subtitle,
        auteur and *sturmendrang,*
and only one or two of us didn't look like hell
        all the time so we were
well-suited, reveling in the *oeuvre* of misery.
        We would say: here's
where you'll be in 10 years, 20 years and it was
        far away and far from
each other—the future as we understood it
        was something, someone
else, event versus increment recruiting us
        for purpose unknown

though we could not imagine the new
        bodies, faces, names
that would replace us: could they replace us?
        We would trust
each other, lie, lose each other, we would watch
        each other change
but you look the same to me now as then—
        keep in mind
how bad my eyes are, astigmatic, my myopia
        simpatico to lines
sketched in forehead and jowl by life lived
        with insouciance, neglect
and torrid behavior inviting more of the same.
        And we said, the door's
always open, which it was because fear
        didn't have anything
we wanted. We wanted. We would light a cigarette
        and sit on the back porch
of fourth-floor walk-ups and the smoke scrawled
        our fates in serif curls,
enlisting sky as tablet, stars as punctuation
        and when direction knocked
we turned up the volume, and when obligation
        ("whose name we do not care
to recall") called, we studiously ignored it
        and when we were smart,
we were very smart, indeed—toeing the line
        between earnest and florid—
and when we were not, we were, wrote Longfellow,
        rhyme-laden bastard
serenading his lovely daughter, horrid.

TUESDAY

If the sky at dusk resembles
the most predictable of pastel landscapes,
it's not my fault.

Stenciled trees flatter
the horizon, piqued by curious light.
We are fettered by vision, but I would not choose
liberation. Maybe, libation.

Streetlights are diplomats, negotiating
the borders of darkness.
I am tired of myself, as you must be. That's why

God rested: He could not stand it
another minute, and so created company.
The angels are lousy at gin, and can't
finish a sentence: some sort of disorder.

The branches, their complications—
vanish. Cars are lens and grill. We must get
used to disappearing. The stars

compete for our affection.
Did I mention my strong prescription?
Every day you become
more attractive.

CIRCUS

We pass a huge tent with turrets
on our way to grandma's house.
There is no wolf, here, no cape or hood.
Only ornate horses, beery clowns, happy
family acrobats, vendors of ferocity.
I tell my children: the circus has three rings.
The only parents who told their kids anything,
when I was growing up, were groovy.
They were pals, confidantes.
They did not embarrass their children,
as is a parent's obligation.

I want my children to tell me everything.
My hearing is considerably better than my husband's:
he's troubled by ambient noise.
I hear the air move: the particles chatting.
I hear the chair say to the table: what's new?
The plaid says to the stripe: I am the pattern here.
A shoelace yearning to be tied.
The little fricatives at the end of sentences.
Unintended sighs.
Please don't confuse hearing with listening.
I did not say: I am a good listener.

These are entirely different skill-sets,
as the marketing geniuses say.
I can spell "Mississippi" very quickly,
do a time-step, thumb wrestle.
Sing "Surrey with the fringe on top" and question
my faith in the decency of human nature
both at the same time.

I can drive with my knees, leaving my hands
free to gesture at neighboring vehicles.
When the right-hand mirror talks to the distance, it says:
I know you are closer than you look.

The distance is taciturn.
Its tactic: emotional blackmail.
The silent treatment.
There's salt back there.
In 1963, my Uncle Denny heard a young
Barbra Streisand audition in a club in downtown Detroit.
You knew she was a star. A star, he said.
I was entranced by the mobile, pictures
of ducks that swayed above my head.
I was not a child of the '60s
but a child in the '60s.

Prepositions make all the difference.
As does "this" versus "that."
As do articles: "A" versus "the."
The general versus the particular.
The random versus the chosen.
A clown is scary. The clown is scary.
We sit in the dark to watch the spectacle.
We sit in the dark. We think about doing our taxes.
The shapes and lights travel across our line
of vision, after the source is gone.
It's an optical trick, but a good one.

I hate magicians. And like all sensible people, mimes.
In a brief, desperate time, I dated
a professional funnyman.
A clown, of sorts.
My relationship with humor has become quite strained.
I can barely stand wit.
Even charm is suspect, if it sneaks up on you.

I don't carry mace but once I did in a dream.
Of course, my attacker turned it on me
and I woke up failing to see.
I woke myself up by screaming.

If you were that funny, they used to call you
a "scream."
My daughter woke up, screaming.
Children are born mimics.
They can build a wall with their hands
without any bricks, and almost lose control
of a balloon, and find chewing gum on their heels
with expressions too big for their faces.
When they call your husband's name, you hear
the shrillness
in your own voice.

HOW TO MAKE THE FAMILIAR STRANGE

Leave your house at aubade-time:
the streetlights still on nightshift, signs
defiantly bright in the font of optimism.
San Bernadino mountains still assume
their position of prominence, yet to
recede in the climate of commerce.
We are speaking, now, to those who
live here and they nod

                              yes, yes

I know just the vista, up Jamboree where Eagle
Scouts plodded decades ago with visions
of orange and strawberry reward, uniform
groves' glut of Edenic succulence,
but it is wherever you live, sky stingy
with light refusing to outline object.

                              how poor a painter is dawn

Before the taxi, slide on your pants—
they are cool and popular. Your shoes,
forgiving. These are pleasant turns of event

                              pluralize "turns" like
                              "sisters-in-law"—
                              the "s" strangely assigned

what with the relentless intrusion
of species-free birds distinguishing
ash from poppy seed by your daughter's

eaves. Local streets are named for trees
beginning in A, B, C: Acacia, Bamboo, Ceiba

you get the idea

the builder's wife an amateur horticulturalist,
amateur Romantic with a jones for taxonomy—
neighborhoods need a logic or each self-
absorbed lane goes its own way and you
can't get anywhere from else

*cul-de-sac, for those who don't
speak film noir: dead end with a
chain-link fence, meager shrubs,
chronically employed poor postures,
everything "slung," "sluggish,"
slowed by adjectives,
inert from lack of action*

Yours has enough

action

and two well-placed parks, cacophony
of shapes for graduating gross motor
skills and children bedeck the metal
until darkness nibbles their ankles,
their great talent to ignore all beacons

*mama's voice in searching timbre,
chill that turns shine to matte, chime
of faux Big Ben at neo-Classical
High*

and though to some this sounds like hell

routine is not my hobgoblin, won't
betray my whereabouts to the mirrored
cops of complacency. So much everyday
snake-charming, baths in nectar, talking
hummingbirds and an incessant good
attitude—the strange familiar my usual
tense, toads and pearls of suburbia,

real estate, school board,
boob job, country club

grouse and praise in the semaphores
of beach umbrellas, code in crumbling
coffeecake, young boys' crop circle haircuts
and the pleasing coincidence of one
ex-wife almost running down the other
in the Ferraried supermarket parking lot.

I didn't see her

When I left, my children beat their breasts;
I hear their keening states away. When back,
we will delight in a normal red wagon and
the brain's capacity to forget

a gift in moderation,
curse in excess

And what will I bring them from my travels?
Looks, brains, unfashionable kindness,
a pitching arm, the antidote to indifference,
a rescue, a molar, a cure, a shard,

a peal of bells ineffable

and for myself, three wishes that don't
backfire like those fabled desires to undo

one always used up wishing
to know what to wish for

the previous folly,
entirely selfish or selfless

no more poverty, no more war,
five flawless carats emerald
cut in a platinum setting

and a pair of fabulous specs to help read
the contractual print below "Drink This"
and so elect the potion's consequence as,
with only mild consternation,

the airplane enters ambivalence,
the ground a visible fiction
as we inch through clouds
the shape of before

"before" -- two syllables Eve
invented in the privacy of exile

damn that snake

I grow tiny and vast.

PERFECTION LETTERS

Share a dish of dried figs with Plato, and he will take them all.

Diogenes

You were way too competent.

Sure, we liked how you lined up the bunnies on the chalkboard ledge to demonstrate Kant's famous "one follows another" theory but that can't compensate for your obsession with historical perspective—you'd think 1921 was yesterday!—or your refusal to tour the plant just because of some adamantine child labor laws.

Your tendency to answer the questions asked can only be viewed as a denial of nuance and near-death experience, something vital to this department's conversation.

If you must know, your bearing was regal and since we are all descended from peasants, the impulse to press our lips to your signet was almost overwhelming.

When you left, the senior committee member kept singing the first baritone part of Handel's "Messiah," which you kazooed through the entire interview.

We found this all too alluring and several bathed soon after.

One turned into a pig.

The way you gestured was truly off-putting—pretending to putt whenever you made a point. That several of us golf biweekly and hang autographed pictures of Jack Nicklaus above the Xerox made the chair want to follow you home and smother you.

We told him: a nice letter will do fine.

(11)

You were way too confident.

And oh! The way you dress: there's a NASCAR driver's second wife missing her tube-top jumpsuit.

Your posture left nothing to be desired, and on desiring you, we eliminated you from the running due to a conflict of interest never to be pursued but that cannot be ignored.

Do you want to go out sometime?

We found strange your way of speaking—as though in translation, and you grew up in several Midwestern towns purchased by movie stars.

Your decision to assume a variety of dialects in the course of a very long sentence was impressive but what did you hope to prove?

Your calligraphic gifts did not go unnoticed—how lovely of you to make place cards!

And with our names in that faux Cyrillic serif?

That turned a few heads, and I thought you might have a chance if not for that obsequious joke about string theory.

The uproarious laughter—I hope you didn't take that as a good sign.

When you spoke of your shoes having windows—then, I thought, you might be onto something, but without my Palm Pilot all figure escapes me—why talk about the soul at a time like this?

Next time, try being more ordinary or exceptional.

Your gloves?

They were catastrophic.

(III)

On close examination, we discovered some discrepancies
on your curriculum vitae that cannot be ignored, though
we are prepared to ignore them, for a price—for example,

what exactly did you mean by "king"? Is there a crest
or sceptre? How do you spell theater? Did a constituency
support your candidacy, or is the criteria one of strict

inheritance? Were you a lovable monarch
or the type who ate all the peasants' eggs for breakfast?
When you say "adept" at overture and showtune,

does that imply the ability to sight-read music, or pleasant
humming as though you only recently forgot the lyrics?
Do you then drum your palps and drift off, like so?

Where did you train as a hand model? Did the big agencies
consider your missing half-digit an asset or debit?
What's your position on the forging of signatures?

You seem to be overqualified for this position --
where did you learn to hotwire a deuce coupe?
Which personality is present today? Can she teach

Medieval Women's Studies and Science 101:
June bugs, Lightning bugs, Mealy bugs—friend or foe?
In summary, when you say "burglar" do you mean

"thief" as in felon with fingerprint rolled side to side
and sullen, everything-has-lead-me-to-this mugshot
or the more metaphoric someone who seeks, finds
and takes what she wants?

(IV)

I'm afraid the position is no longer available—
our program has been purged of funds for those
teaching the core curriculum of push-pin
creation and how to twist balloons

into garden gnomes and gendarmes. We cannot
even offer our standard course in ice sculpting!
So you see, we could not hire you unless
you were willing to work for a stipend

of generous yet inappropriate
affection. After the wholesale looting
of our supply room, all we could offer by way
of equipment is one tripod and an intercom.

After you earned some respect, you could snap
the class picture—bring film from home.
The one vestige of dignity remaining is our
palace and its staff. Cook is famous for

her quail! And the faculty cannot survive
without one stout butler. As a new hire,
your perquisites would include a key
to the pedestrian washroom, which you can see

from the glass elevator in Tower III, where
you would "let down your hair." Your classes
would be held in caves, where acoustics suit
a sotto voce delivery, so best bring your Poe

along with your thigh-high waders
and a miniature blow-torch, the best kind
for keeping bats upside down and browning
the top of a nice crème brulee.

(V)

When you said,
"my hand is a stanza"
it really offended some
of the committee

so we felt justified in
cutting it off without
anesthesia, and felt you
responded poorly

to mutilation. Teaching
is no easy berth, my dear purser!
The fact that you are a mother
was looked upon without favor

when you offered to make
peanut butter and jelly sandwiches
for faculty lunches.
Surely you know that we are

a peanut-free facility! Nonetheless,
you were this close
(I am now holding a bagel
between thumb and forefinger

to indicate the inch between
employment and your despair)—
indeed, this would have been a
fine position for you, someone

who appreciates a student body
schooled in the nuances of secret
handshake, password and ritual
hazing: don't dunk when drunk!

Haven't you learned by now? If not
for the committee member
who swears you dated his brother
and dumped him, I quote,

"like a goddam hot potato,"
we would have reacted to you
favorably—I can't compliment
that interview suit enough,

but the shoes—
what were you thinking?
How could a pump possibly
be appropriate in time of war

or during the gymnastics floor exercise?
Next time, choose a nice
sling-back. This makes us understand:
you are serious, incapable

of containing your passion
for scholarship within the confines
of your body. A reminder:
we like a *soupcon*

of interpretive dance—it reminds
us of our youth in the circus,
when we ate fire
and wore a nose.

(VI)

Two of us were duly impressed when you applied that tourniquet and debunked the pathetic fallacy but that does not change the fact—your area does not suit our needs: we already have a specialist in dead tongues and we find him, frankly, a little macabre. Imagine the two of you at faculty meetings eating mutton or manna or ludovisc, trading quips—ha! ha!—we don't want that kind of exclusivity in this apartment. We prefer to snub for personal reasons, and often ask candidates to reveal something intimate, a terrible secret to be used only in emergencies: sordid is best, an investigation where someone is called upon to be "good cop." Did you know that "thumbs up" in Roman times meant, "kill him"? How that became a symbol of approbation is beyond us, and classicists are so damn unbearable, we refuse to eat their crusts and curd. Take your papyrus and columns. Go sulk like Antigone before she was lowered into that hole in the rocks—a lot of good that attitude did her.

(VII)

Your recommendations could not have been any stronger:

one mentor praised your ability to keep his goldfish alive during a troubling divorce; another trumpeted your gifts with papier mache and gouache.

How transgressive!

One letter, however, compared your code of ethics to that of Hammurabi's assassins—what to make of this? Did you smash her car or slay her prize heifer? We understand that you are family but best keep internecine squabbles out of the application process.

(Just a tip.) (From a "Friend.")

Your syllabi, however, stun: that course you developed on "Conversation in the Shapes of Hello Kitty and Those Squiggles of Kandinsky"

What a reading list!

We also enjoyed, "Tribal Conflict: *Handbag v. Pocketbook*" and know our students would benefit from the pursuit, "mano a mano."

When you measured each of us with that retractable tape, we thought it a bit odd until you explained its relevance to the notion that the righteous should surround themselves with righteousness—

isn't that Maimonides?

Aren't you ashamed?

And with the exception of your extradition to another state on "trumped up" federal charges, your recommendations—contrary to some systems of belief, we do not all have all day and plans in the desert—

could not have been any longer.

(VIII)

The senior v.p. in charge of h.r.
was somewhat "p.o.'ed" at your
unwillingness to express an opinion
on Rodgers and Hammerstein v.
Rodgers & Hart and you refused
to take the chair's cues (the blatant
"cut off your head" gesture) and
pursued this line of discussion
when the woman was emphatic
that "I Could Have Danced All Night"
was unimpeachable. This apparent
inability to "suck up" might make you
a heavyweight contender in some green
departments but we are past
our salad days and need a sworn
oath to the platform. Your research
was quixotic but friendly—who knew
Milton an Albino? Brahms longed
for a bicycle?—and your cover "note"
of one syllable per line persuaded
some that the virtue of patience
should be lodged in the circular file
(eddy of glorious failures) between
sloth and slovenliness.

You've never seen death? Look in the mirror every day
and you will see it like bees working in a glass hive.

Jean Cocteau

THE INTERVIEW

Why did you leave your previous position?
I heard a rumor of blurring.
I heard you learned to refract the light

so it would not attack
so sharply.
You thought she would be grateful? She was

grateful
that you applied a poultice of lies.
A better balm than trust.

Listen here:
I won't have a houseful of you
working the angles.

And what if the glass got all soft
like gauze, and I stepped through . . .
Implausible.

How do you like professional vanity?
So Ecclesiastical—you must get tired
of hearing that.

I get tired of dancing in red-hot boots.
Some days, I just fall off
a cliff into the yielding sea....

Beauty is no curse.
Beauty is a spell, a divine error, dividing
inside from out

and what is "good" and "true"
resides where?
But spells wear off and what's worse

than the poison of nostalgia? Face and frame
reimbursed so cruelly by time.
Time emits a foul smell, if you ask me.

Who is to blame for my plight?
I like only the truths I like. Canaries in the mine
were not rewarded with fame.

I tightened her bodice.
Untangled her hair.
Fed her an apple.

One apple, one wish. One death, one prince.
Doesn't that sound fair?
What can compare with a mother's love?

Let me read to you a tale:
"The typical mirror is a sheet of glass
with a thin layer of molten aluminum or silver

sputtered on the back."
The typical mother raises her daughter
to be as she imagines herself

and so my failure was one of imagination.
The literal suffer so.
Who looks at a mirror to see a mirror?

Adieu, for the beans are ripe.
Behave yourself: I could get a wise, bonny trout.
Or a doll, a knife, and a pumice stone.

Seven robbers and an oxcart.
A helpful eagle
and chambermaids.

Oh, wash me with water and wine
and fetter me in finery.
                         Forgiveness—that's another story.

FAIRYTALE SMALLTALK

This tulle-and-taffeta prom dress of a morning makes promises it can't keep.

    A bird orange as

(analogy finds nothing in nature, counts to ten and goes searching for)

redemption or your new sweater

competes with the coral tree's flower-seed for the free—

floating attention of a wandering eye and I tell my brother:

    I am that bird.

He says: look yourself up in the guide and tell me what you are.

I reply: I am an orange-throated tanager.

He says: that's unlikely, you're nowhere near Peru, you're

    a finch or an oriole.

Indifferent to identity, I become a rose thorn and spy a finger

                      nearing me—

    so this is how the spindle feels.

WE TALK ABOUT ROSES

My compliments on
the self-defense mechanism:
today when my daughter
presented me with a clump
of 18 clothed in cellophane,
one token branch and
a baby's breath to interrupt
the Nebuchadnezzar of red,

I nearly bled to death
while cutting off the bottom
three inches and stripping
leaves from below the vase's
water-line: I have never encountered
so many thorns in one place
and by the time nine were ready
for submersion there was

one part blood to three parts water
and mildly dizzy I muttered,
only a flesh-wound, did I sign up
for human sacrifice? and
what price, pulchritude? Pricked over
and over by the spindle
of flora, I suppose beauty needs
certain advantages in order to

protect itself from natural predators:
those in love, those lovelorn,
lost loves, those less
blessed with loveliness.

A YEAR ON MARS

is nearly twice as long as a year
on Earth. It takes the Red Planet

687 Earth days to circle the sun—
nearly as long as I orbited you

before I began to degenerate.
You must be awfully affable,

having befriended time—and such
a flamboyant wardrobe! Remember

our first date? An illustrated lecture
on the sex lives of ancient Romans?

You learned that I am no classicist—
can't tell an urn from a cistern,

column from ruin and slept through
the dawn of the sundial. I discovered

the duration of a perfect year:
according to Plato, 36,000 years,

his calculations ideal, at best.
That would have been some courtship!

Thus began the infancy of our détente,
when I stopped wearing isinglass and

eyelet and began this igneous adventure.
During lunch hours, to please you,

I searched for a true red, an *ipse dixit*
ipso facto. During the Iron Age, a period

of ruddiness that I recall only vaguely
as this low-carb diet affects short-term

memory, everyone was annoyed, hurling
invectives and bumping into the sun

while waves swarmed the shore: not the idyll
you detailed in your notorious memoir

and I am not that palled, triple-jointed
lass stranded on that mythic isthmus.

I was always called upon to break
through the line—*Red Rover, Red Rover*—

because I was bloodless, cool to the touch.
How long it takes to say, "ice…"—

nearly a full year on Mars with that
tall drink of a vowel and lazy sibilant.

At this rate, we shall need Plato's full
allotment to know what each other

is capable of—stranding a preposition,
widowing a noun—while Mission Control

is still giving orders and perfection is
                            so far away.

THE PAIN OF PRODUCE

The grass looks happy today.
Some days it seems bereft.

I feel guilty staking the claim on emotion.
There are people who believe that fruits and vegetables scream when harvested.
That plants have feelings.

Isn't "harvest" a nice word?

Myself, I don't subscribe to the verdant pain of produce.
I went to a school for the gifted and talented.
Our punishments were mostly self-inflicted.

We tended to prick our fingers on spindles.
Went to class in geodesic domes, painted pastel.
And in a great mansion, not unlike a castle.

There was a creek and legend of the man across it with a shotgun.
I knew he was a legend because he never aged, transcending time like some tome.

The gifted and talented are gullible.
We would cross the creek: everyone likes manageable danger.
Our code was no different: the weak will pay.
Who is weak: not always apparent.

The treehouse was the real torture-chamber, home of truth-or-dare.
None of my strategies worked.
The truths cried out, the dares were merciless.
A Darwinian game, like Red Rover: I ran back and forth, of no use.
In earlier times, I may not have survived.

If not for that slice of countryside, nature would be foreign to me
as those small countries—Andorra, Monaco, Luxembourg.
I traveled into the steep, snowy hills of San Marino on a bus tour.
We gave the country a single day.
On the bus, I was fairly sure I would not be returning.

Ominous ice and
the snow did not look happy.

Not like small-town snow: authentic.
Or city snow: the least of one's problems.

It looked sinister, the way some cul-de-sacs do.
That's French for "sack-bottom"
and the only outlet is the entrance.

Militarily, this is where you want to be, unless you are the army
hemmed in on all sides except behind.

Nearing this in the dictionary are "cul-de-lampe" and "cul-de-four"—
the lamp and the furnace, respectively.
There's that famous book *The Mirror and the Lamp*

that explains a great deal about Romanticism, which we miss.
We loved nature so: it was an ameliorating presence.

Toxic nostalgia.

I spent years living in a dictionary.
It was a hospitable domicile.
When I left, I was shocked

at the temperature
inside and outside
and the way the plums talked to each other

inside their dark bag
inside the Frigidaire.

CUL-DE-SAC

House 1.
My neighbor would like me to write about
what we
(ALL OF US) (THE LADIES) (IN MY NEIGHBORHOOD)
know. She feels we are under-
represented in art, though I tell her:
no one is getting
represented these days, though
we could be recorded
in portraiture, were we
wealthy, beautiful, or odd.
(SOME OF US ARE ONE OR MORE OF THESE.)

Here is what we think about:
silent, kidney-shaped pools
bad seeds, lying (THEIRS) (OURS)
steeply rising property values
the hypotenuse between ballet and swim class
enough
whether heaven has marble or hard-wood floors
the uncertainty principal
a lost child, chaos theory

(A LOST CHILD)
Stop!
(THINKING ABOUT THINGS THAT WON'T HAPPEN)
(BECAUSE WE ARE VIGILANT)(AND LUCKY)(BECAUSE WE
MUST BE).

House 2.
My neighbor sweeps
her arm grandly and points
fingers: here there are private sales on designer
bags and shoes and free-
floating despair on clearance rounders
and parties where one sad story skirts
the perimeter and there is pity
and greed, compassion and fear and faith lost
and found and when
did you get so holy? And how

did you get so skinny?
There is an extra bed and bath
for the imagination, a Jacuzzi and plush
towels for the muse and if you think
that couple of sad abstractions
doesn't like comfort,
guess again: polish up
the sterling, break out

the Bordeaux and let it breathe
in a goblet big as ambition
where wine expands to its full
expense.

House 3.
My neighbor wonders what we
(THE LADIES)

have in common. I tell her: we all
solve our problems while the shower
absolves us with wetwhite noise:
how to fix a
(POEM)(MARRIAGE)(SPRINKLER)
          correct a flaw in
(CHARACTER)(CASSEROLE).
And fear, I tell her, fear
connects us, though it's no innoculation.

And our questions are similar
to the mid-day questions of our mid-century mothers:
why is door number two
always a mule, door number one
an appliance, and door number three
an ingénue who played Eliza
Doolittle in the third touring company
wearing a Cubic Zirconia?
If I can come, and I probably can't,
can I bring a friend?

House 4.
My neighbor thinks
we are not thinking well.
In the swingset of the mind, she starts
to say (PUMP, PUMP!)—I interrupt:

a little philosophy in each lunchbox will do
nicely, and some science in the thermos.
Rousseau believed in man's "perfectibility,"
Sartre thought our freedom terrifying, Spinoza
bade free will *adieu,* and Pythagoras
said that we are not the center
of the universe, though the odds
of raising children to err on the side of
compassion are nearly a million to one,
and worse if you get them
shiny, new bikes for their birthdays.

(WHICH WE DO.) (AND MORE.)
In their baskets, they carry
small tokens of privilege that they barter
for magic beans, freedom

from our protection, from our
spurned friendship with the world.

(ARE YOU SURE YOU CAN'T STAY?)

House 5.
My neighbor disapproves of
digression and while we're at it,
secular tendencies. I tell her: daily, we recite

the prayer to Elijah, the children's prophet:
Please let their lives be better, longer
than mine and he is inscrutable,
never a sip of wine, never a sign.
(CAN'T YOU GIVE ME A SIGN?)
In Eden, God did not curse
the child—then, adults were as children,
naked of guile until guilt
tracked them down and
the Black Forest witches
gave each princess 16 years head-start

before lacing love with poison
and giving them a good night's sleep.
Yeats prayed for just enough—not too much—
beauty for his daughter,
("... THE STRANGER'S EYE DISTRAUGHT")
and we would not wish for
beauty without purpose,
though they make a shocking, sweet pair.
We do not know what to wish for
(FOR THEM)(FOR US)

except time. Plato liked his measured
in heavenly bodies
(MEET ME AT THE SUMMER SOLSTICE)
but what did he know
of a day the duration of a year,
and years shouting back over their shoulders,
don't wait up. Back then, time was kooky,
it hardly passed except during wars
and orations.

House 6.
My neighbor does not find
this explanation satisfactory. She taps a manicured
Morse code on my Travertine countertop.

I take her out for a coffee and say:
when the furies fly up and buzz
around your head once you open the hatbox
of fate, do as Pandora did: love them
and want them to go away
until after they've had a bath, their hair
dries smelling of lavender and lavishly
buttered toast. Mumble
the story about walking to school
clutching a baked potato to keep you
warm (YOU ATE IT FOR LUNCH)

(AND WHAT OF THE WALK HOME?)
of having only a tire swing, a cousin
and a pony to play with
(AND WE WERE SO DAMN HAPPY)
(WEREN'T WE?)
and answer to No One
who always makes requests at dawn,
in the presence of dew, or manna, or quail,
or all of the above,
because (I SAID SO)
because (THE SOUL RETURNS TO THE BODY)
because (IS ENOUGH OF A REASON).

ROSES: CHAPTER TWO

When at night you cut
the corner and see
stars, they are lovely—
in a semi-conscious
sort of way. Even
the crows here are
afflicted with it—
beauty, I mean—I am
ever-startled by
some flash of underwing.
The tire-swing suspended
from its green chain,
the indelicate gravel
that reveals the presence
of the man come to
read the meter—none
are exempt, gorgeous
to the core. Roses
must compete and so
sulk, aim their thorns
at mortal judges.
The pain both quick
and sustaining.

YOU AND DEANNA DESERVE EACH OTHER

I am sorry that you recognized yourself.
It was bound to happen.
My sources of grief and inspiration: beaus, foes,
people who have wronged me,
people who have done such a nice turn that I do not forget.
In this way, I am like my mother.
It once pained me to admit that.
But you see, I am mature now.
She hardly shows up in my work.
She's too busy, and I don't want to bother her.
You know, you have to entertain people when you use them.
Put out some coffeecake and Danish.

I made you up.
You didn't do those heroic things I mentioned.
You don't look as hot as I described.
My mother says I remember so much.
Unfortunately, this is ironic: we're hardly chronicled at all,
unlike those people who trace family trees back to Cro-Magnon times.
And they are so proud of it!
I am from hearty peasant stock from Minsk or Pinsk, but every now and then
my mother tries to float something about
her grandfather being a general in the Russian army.
This is highly unlikely; a wished-for fiction.
It would explain a great deal.

You know how Coleridge was interrupted by the doorbell as he recorded Kubla
Khan from his dream?
That just happened.
And I was on the verge of brilliance.
It was a wrong number: a kind-sounding woman asked for Deanna.

There's no Deanna here, I said. Just you and my mother.
She's busy entertaining the afterlife.
Making a nice brisket.
Maybe I will use Deanna.
Maybe that's her penance for my loss.
I will turn her into someone who kicks dogs and bullies her children.
Or a saint. A goddamn saint.

I will turn her into you.
That will show both of you.

SALTON SEA

For Syd & Will

The shallow basin of the Salton Sea,
        haven for fish, bugs and salinity,

attracts birds like flies, flies like opposites—
        those wayward pairs—opposites like bees

to honey, and there, comparison takes
        a well-deserved hiatus as some things can't be

likened to other things in that good spirit
        of fellowship, cauldron where we all get along

"in the soup." Imagination bonds the worlds
        we witness and invent and so the dolly

that can hardly hold her eyes open she's so
        weary of her faux-porcelain veneer, earns

free will, a name, a role, often found
        come morning near the door. If I have

a soul-mate in this universe of ideas
        larded with syllable, it is eschatology,

study of the end of the world, as I cannot resist
        thoughts of the worst, how I'd perish

in a truly Victorian fashion without you,
        the way that—why pause, as though I am

considering options when none suffice.
I should adopt the magnolia's ideology—

folding beauty, slow-motion descent and
demise, though I was raised to be estranged

from nature and resent her lessons, lousy
pedant. I prefer road to green, vehicle

to bloom, and I, nor you, are anything
like a machine, despite politic mumblings

of cogs—you can say cog over and over
but it does not make you round, notched

and oily. So when I see the motorcyclist
legally, blithely navigating the carpool lane

I think, he must contain a multitude,
like Whitman, he must contradict himself

and his parts need have nothing in common
save cooperation to proceed due north. If we are lonely

it's for destination, the middle-class cousin
of destiny, which prefers to fly in a J-shaped

echelon, trailing luck, flanked by fate
and the contrary, as there can be no progress

without tension, said Blake and I believe him.
The Salton Sea relies on man at his

eco-worst: aggie run-off, stagnant pools,
no rain to sweeten the pot, too far inland

for property to count while migratory
        tourists, with better than human names—

eared grebe and the yuma clapper rail—
        ("threatened" we are told by do-gooders)

touch down at their favorite stinky resort.
        The rider puts up his feet, Apollo

with a muffler doctored so we will know
        he exists—I bike, therefore I am—

figure of leisure, of speed, skimming
        the divider stripes, no plaguing penchant

for connection beneath a sky that makes
        no guarantees, and so must be trusted.

STICK & STONES

I met a small boy named Ari and told him his name
meant lion so he should have courage,
but this scared him away.
Bishop Berkeley believed all material objects
and space and time, an illusion.
As does my mother-in-law.
We get along famously.

I told the boy's mother, if this is true, your young son
should not fear me
or my smattering of knowledge.
When she stops picketing my home
I will tell her what Dr. Johnson did when told of Berkeley's opinion.
He cried: "I refute it thus!" and stubbed his toe
on a large stone.

Still, the ladies of Newport do not care for me and my
vision of child-raising:
make the child invent
a song of leaves each morning, a song of mourning
each night as they cower beneath their eaves,
clutching a small branch. When you meet
the devil in a dream, I tell my son,

poke him in the eye.
My grandmother said: if a man lifts his hand
to strike you, break his arm.
We are punitive people.
The word for viola in German is "bratsche"—literally, arm.
"Give me a hand" is my favorite example of synecdoche.
There are 19 bones in the hand, my favorite extremity.

My favorite stories star princesses and tiny men.
Sometimes the tiny men want what they cannot have—
often the princess.
Other times they have limited expectations:
a rock or two to play with,
or gratitude, which is often limited.
My favorite films are stories of someone

who has amnesia and discovers
a previous life in which she was royalty
with cleavage. Or films about the future
where everyone wears tunics
and owns personal hover-crafts,
never getting their feet wet as water smothers
the earth and people gather atop hills

with olive branches clenched
in their jaws, performing talents that would put
pageant contestants to shame.
Pick me! Pick me! shout the sarongs.
And the gods, who go unnamed
since names can hurt you, choose a few to repopulate
the earth. This time, everyone

a winner, with no ambition and brave to the core.
I like films that star the comely
Jean-Paul Belmondo.
He is my favorite illusion.
He speeds in a coupe and tips his hat
at fate. In my vision, we skip French stones
and get along famously.

CATASTROPHE IS A HARD BLOW

All questions of science, contingent.

Take catastrophe. How many feet would the oceans need to rise to rate such a title? This depends on your vision of ends. One more foot: a floodplain deluged. Three more could devastate the Mekong Delta. If you have Noah phobia, do not worry: including the polar icecaps, there's not enough water on earth to cover even half of the planet's dry land. Even half! If everything melted. I'm sure your pair would be arid. You'd be waving from atop Mount Ararat.

Take heat. If the body is 98.6 degrees inside, why lament the temperature outside? This depends on your vision of perception—a feverishly debated issue. Networks of brain and nerve, the skin's receptors gauge the ambient and make you feel hot before you have a right. You drink, you sweat, you slow your endeavors. By hook or crook, the body gets its fix, tells consciousness: take a seat, pal. *What a piece of work is man.* Truly, darling, you are that piece.

Take stars. You search them out in a navy night. What makes you see them after a hard blow to the head? This depends on your vision of visions. The experts have some ideas: cortex and lobe, brainpain—the seat of sensation. Phosphenes deluge the floodplain. Do you complain, or map the constellations? Wish them away, or petition to stay them? Even half such stars could fill the firmament before the governing charges abated and you saw nothing.

(I have been a fool for less.)

HOUSE BRAND

Yesterday, a man named Stephen Alternative
wed a nice girl with the last name, Smith.

She became Barbara Alternative.

What would it be like to be forever the other?

My name remained my own.

I know—don't tell me—it's my father's name. I am still steeped in the
patriarchy yeah yeah yeah and worse,
a named shortened from endless Eastern European glottal syllabics for what
shtetl from which we hailed or the blue-collar profession my ancestors
performed with such integrity
to satisfy the homogeny police.

Tell me again, with a sharp stick: I should have chosen a new name
in some uncorrupted language
but I stuck with the status quo
because Latin holds up well, over time.

I thought everyone would do this.

I meant to fit in.

It backfired.

I have a lot of dinner parties and try to invite people
not like me, not like each other.

No one has a very good time, but no one leaves early,
out of fear they will be the subject of chortling.

At home in bed, they think glad thoughts
about the course of their lives and when they turn off
the lights and the moon turns on, they say aloud,
Hello, Nothingness, Where Have You Been Hiding?

AUBERGINE

I am developing the bad habit of wanting
                    to discuss with my friends the stuff
          philosophers entertain at odd hours, drinking
          absinthe, over-

looking the Neva or in prison for
          thinking, but my impulse occurs at a tony
            restaurant, the atmosphere half-opium den,
          half-tea-at-the-manor

named, so says the rehearsed maitre 'd, after
                  the French word for eggplant, though I am
          impartial to eggplant. So I bring up
          time, how it seems to be

eluding me, not the fact of it
          but the idea—I just can't get it—and my friends,
            who looked happy when we drove up, now look
      weary, as though they'd just finished

a 15-mile training run or reached the first
                  base-camp with no Sherpa
          in sight. And I am trying to figure out
            "confit" and "emulsion," the parts

of animals I did not know,
                  animals I did not know were options
            for consumption, which course
          comes first, the rotation

of utensils, water—tap, bottled, bubbled

or *senza gas*—and we choose a wine
more complex than a soul, its nuances deserving several
doctoral dissertations

and probably a parade, a vintage
I try to taste with every part
of my tongue so it will not feel wasted
on me though so much effort implies

that I am an earnest swine sniffing
pearls and swigging the gems
clumsily from a goblet
the size of my prodigious snout. So my friend's husband,

who finds me annoyingly
likable, says, *well, if you must know,*
Hesiod used natural phenomena—solstice and equinox—
to delineate periods of time and his wife, among my

dearest friends,
chips in, *Thales of Miletus predicted*
the eclipse that would terrify General Nicias
170 years later. Before I can say, *huh?* my husband gently

chides,
He was lucky. Anaxagoras was the first
to really understand that the earth blocked
the moon from the sun's light and at this point,

our appetizers arrive, they are tiny, fragrant,
geometric, orbiting a bowl
of dipping sauce and I notice that plates
look a lot like moons, or clocks, and the waiter says,

yes, I've been thinking
        about this—did you know Anaximander felt time
                the great equalizer? And the suntanned head
        of a Human Relations department at the table to our right proceeds

to break a wooden chair in half
                over the Art Nouveau fountain,
        pries off two slats from the back and demonstrates
the ancient gnomon, used to cast

shadows that could be measured
                to gauge the passage of time. I have finished
                        my first two glasses of wine and am swirling
                the third furiously in the bell

when the owner comes over,
                about to thank us, I think, for spending
                        an entire paycheck at his establishment. Instead,
                        he pulls up a (metal) chair,

the kind you find littering Parisian
                street cafes and elbows on
                        the table, confides,
                Xenophon believed the ecliptic to be oblique and his wife says,

wasn't he Socrates' disciple? and everyone
                nods so I nod like crazy. Fortunately,
                        our main courses are ready—did someone really
        order a pig?—"Glazed pig!" says the chef,

who also ferries a fish from another
                        hemisphere and a platter of something entirely
        brined and when I am sure the meal will resume
                        its cycle and talk will turn

to the kids' foibles, a dabble of politics and local
                              theatre, the chef asks,
          Is everything alright? and my companions laugh
                    and chorus,

Considering Euxodus' flawed theory
                    of concentric spheres! That brings
                    the sous-chef out of the kitchen
          and the pastry chef, visiting that evening,

from Biarritz, where, as it turns out,
                    she studies the plights of brown dwarf stars,
                         so the talk turns to Plato—of course!
          —and his Theory of the Perfect Year—when all

of the celestial bodies reach
                    their starting point—*whenever that is!*—
                    chortles the busboy. And when the cop riding
                    his bike on the beach-beat comes in and says,

I couldn't help
          overhearing—how naïve to posit the velocity
                              of the earth and moon as constant! and gestures
          for a menu, I think,

this has gotten out of hand.
                    But it's not like I own time, the whole
                    restaurant singing its libretto, an overture
                         of flatware, silverware and crystal,

for all I know, the whole town is mumbling
                         in ancient Greek while some kid covers
                    aging rocker Mick moaning,
          "Time Is On My Side" at a concert on the pier.

I can't take these evenings
            when I realize my subject, my obsession
            so vague I can't even articulate
        a problem, is floating around in the air,

it's oxygen with some nitrous
            oxide thrown in so even breathing near it gives
                a tremendous buzz.
        The waiter is naming constellations, my friend ponders

the creation of the calendar to the cop
            quoting Ecclesiastes and the owner looks
                content as a pasha, reclining
        to show the wealth of the situation, so when I say

my, would you look at the time
            and we have to pay the sitter,
            they look at me kindly, squinting
            as though I were growing smaller, or bigger—I eye

my wine, have the clocks all struck
            thirteen?—or distant, how the imagination
                might fathom
        someone you once knew and grew

away from, someone who managed
            to stay quite still while doing
            a great imitation of progress, someone
        baffled by how, where and why

the evening went and what
            could be done to get it back.

ACKNOWLEDGMENTS

"Cul-de-sac," *At Length*, 2013.

"The Case for Free Will," *Pushcart Prize Anthology 2011*.

"A Year on Mars," Cerise Press 2, no. 5, Fall/Winter 2010.

"Perfection Letters iv, vi." *Parthenon West Review*, 2010.

"Catastrophe is a Hard Blow," *Hotel Amerika*, 2009.

"The Interview," "Salton Sea," *Chaparral*, 2009.

"Days of 1984," "The Case for Free Will," *Arroyo Literary Review*, Spring 2009.

"Stick & Stones (i)," *New Zoo Poetry Review*, no. 12, January 2009.

"Perfecta" and "Stick & Stones (ii)," *Slope*, Summer 2008.

"The Plan for Today," *Diagram*, no. 7.4.

"Perfection Letter (viii)," *Verse Daily*, August 18, 2007, reprinted from 5AM, no. 26, Summer 2007.

"The Pitch," *Verse Daily*, September 4, 2007, reprinted from Cimarron Review, Summer 2007.

"Aubergine," *Verdad* 3, Summer 2007.

"The Pain of Produce," *Askew*, no. 4, Fall/Winter 2007.

"Pathetic Pathetic Fallacy," *No Tell Motel*, October 16, 2006.

"Perfection Letters, 1, 2 and 3," *Oxford Magazine*, no. 20.

"Perfection Letter," *Pleiades*, Spring 2006.

"Perfection Letters vii, viii," *5 AM*, no. 26, Summer 2007.

"You and Deanna Deserve Each Other," *88*, no. 5, October 2005.

"Tuesday," *Swink*, no. 2.

"That Was Then," *Hotel Amerika*, 2009.

"The Pitch," *Cimarron Review*, Summer 2007.

PATTY SEYBURN has published three books of poems, *Hilarity* (New Issues Press, 2009), *Mechanical Cluster* (Ohio State University Press, 2002), and *Diasporadic* (Helicon Nine Editions, 1998). She teaches at California State University, Long Beach, and co-edits *POOL: A Journal of Poetry* (www.poolpoetry.com).

TITLES FROM

WHAT BOOKS PRESS

POETRY

Molly Bendall & Gail Wronsky, *Bling & Fringe (The L.A. Poems)*

Laurie Blauner, *It Looks Worse Than I Am*

Kevin Cantwell, *One of Those Russian Novels*

Ramón García, *Other Countries*

Karen Kevorkian, *Lizard Dream*

Patty Seyburn, *Perfecta*

Judith Taylor, *Sex Libris*

Lynne Thompson, *Start with a Small Guitar*

Gail Wronsky, *So Quick Bright Things*
BILINGUAL, SPANISH TRANSLATED BY ALICIA PARTNOY

ART

Gronk, *A Giant Claw*
BILINGUAL, SPANISH

Chuck Rosenthal, Gail Wronsky, & Gronk,
Tomorrow You'll Be One of Us: Sci Fi Poems

PROSE

Rebbecca Brown, *They Become Her*

François Camoin, *April, May, and So On*

A.W. DeAnnuntis, *Master Siger's Dream*

A.W. DeAnnuntis, *The Final Death of Rock and Roll and Other Stories*

A.W. DeAnnuntis, *The Mermaid at the Americana Arms Motel*

Katharine Haake, *The Origin of Stars and Other Stories*

Katharine Haake, *The Time of Quarantine*

Mona Houghton, *Frottage & Even As We Speak: Two Novellas*

Rod Val Moore, *Brittle Star*

Chuck Rosenthal, *Are We Not There Yet?*
Travels in Nepal, North India, and Bhutan

Chuck Rosenthal, *Coyote O'Donohughe's History of Texas*

Chuck Rosenthal, *West of Eden: A Life in 21st Century Los Angeles*

WHAT
BOOKS
PRESS

LOS ANGELES

What Books Press books may be ordered from:
SPDBOOKS.ORG | ORDERS@SPDBOOKS.ORG | (800) 869 7553 | AMAZON.COM

Visit our website at
WHATBOOKSPRESS.COM

CPSIA information can be obtained
at www.ICGtesting.com
Printed in the USA
FSOW02n1311131014
3242FS